J. Nevett. Steele

Hymns and Carols Set to Music

J. Nevett. Steele

Hymns and Carols Set to Music

ISBN/EAN: 9783337089863

Printed in Europe, USA, Canada, Australia, Japan

Cover: Foto ©Lupo / pixelio.de

More available books at **www.hansebooks.com**

HYMNS AND CAROLS

SET TO MUSIC

BY THE

REV. J. NEVETT STEELE,

RECTOR OF ZION CHURCH, WAPPINGER'S FALLS, NEW YORK.

NEW YORK

JAMES POTT & CO., PUBLISHERS

1889

PREFATORY NOTE.

The author hereby wishes to acknowledge his obligation to Messrs. GEO. WILLIG & CO., Baltimore, Md., for their permission to print the Carols: *"All this night bright angels sing," "Waken Christian children," "On the birthday of the Lord";*

And also to Messrs. WM. A. POND & Co. for use of Carols *"A Child this day is born," "What Child is this?" "On the birthday of the Lord";*

And also to Messrs. GEO. SCHIRMER & Co., for use of Carol *"When Christ was born of Mary free."*

These Carols are copyrighted and may be procured from the publishers.

The other Carols in this book are published for the first time.

THE AUTHOR.

ZION RECTORY,
Advent, 1889.

Easter. Hymn 108.

Words from Hymnal. Music by J. Nevett Steele.

1 Lift your glad voices in triumph on high, For Je - sus hath risen, and
man can-not die. Vain were the terrors that gath-ered a-round him, And
rit. molto. a tempo.
short the dominion of death and the grave; He burst from the fetters of darkness that
bound him, Resplendent in glory to live and to save. Loud was the chorus of
angels on high, "The Saviour hath risen, and man shall not die."

2 Glory to God, in full anthems of joy!
The being he gave us, death cannot destroy;
Sad were the life we must part with to-morrow,
  If tears were our birthright, and death were our end!
But Jesus hath cheered the dark valley of sorrow,
  And bade us, immortal, to heaven ascend.
Lift your glad voices in triumph on high,
Jesus hath risen, and man shall not die.

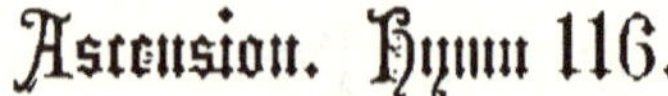

Words from Hymnal. Music by J. Nevett Steele.

CHORUS. *Allegro molto.* *Fine.*

Crown Him! Crown Him! Crown Him with many crowns! Crown Him! Crown Him! Crown Him with many crowns!

Crown Him with ma - ny Crowns! The Lamb up - on His throne. . . . Hark, how the heav'n - ly an - them drowns all mu - sic but its own. A - wake, my soul, and sing . . . . of

rit. *a tempo.* *rit.* *D.C.*

Him who died for thee, . . . and hail Him as thy match-less King, Thro' all e - ter - ni - ty.

2 Crown him the Virgin's Son!
The God incarnate born,
Whose arm those crimson trophies won
Which now his brow adorn.
Fruit of the Mystic Rose,
True Branch of Jesse's stem,
The Root whence mercy ever flows,—
The Babe of Bethlehem!

3 Crown him the Lord of love!
Behold his hands and side,—
Those wounds, yet visible above,
In beauty glorified:
No angel in the sky
Can fully bear that sight,
But downward bends his wondering eye
At mysteries so bright.

4 Crown him the Lord of peace!
Whose power a sceptre sways
In heaven and earth, that wars may cease,
And all be prayer and praise.
His reign shall know no end;
And round his piercèd feet
Fair flowers of Paradise extend
Their fragrance ever sweet.

5 Crown him the Lord of heaven!
One with the Father known,
And the blest Spirit, through him given,
From yonder Triune throne!
All hail, Redeemer, hail!
For thou hast died for me:
Thy praise and glory shall not fail
Throughout eternity.

HYMN 162.

J. N. S.

1. Let me with light and truth be bless'd; Be these my guides to keep the
way, Till on Thy ho - ly hill I rest, And in Thy sa - cred tem-ple
pray: Then will I there fresh al - tars raise To God who is my on - ly
joy; And well-tuned harps, with songs of praise, Shall all my grateful hours employ.

2 Why then cast down, my soul? and why
So much oppressed with anxious care?
On God, thy God for aid rely,
Who will thy ruin'd state repair.
To Father, Son, and Holy Ghost,
The God whom earth and heaven adore,
Be glory as it was of old,
Is now and shall be evermore.

Hymn 169.

Danish Melody.
Arr. by J. N. S.

1. Sav - iour, a - gain to thy dear name we raise,
With one ac - cord, our part - ing hymn of praise:
We stand to bless thee ere our wor - ship cease,
Then, low - ly kneel - ing, wait thy word of peace.

2 Grant us thy peace upon our homeward way;
With thee began, with thee shall end the day;
Guard thou the lips from sin, the hearts from shame,
That in this house have called upon thy name.

3 Grant us thy peace, Lord, through the coming night,
Turn thou for us its darkness into light;
From harm and danger keep thy children free,
For dark and light are both alike to thee.

4 Grant us thy peace throughout our earthly life,
Our balm in sorrow, and our stay in strife;
Then, when thy voice shall bid our conflict cease,
Call us, O Lord, to thine eternal peace.

St. John's Day. Hymn 175.

Words from Hymnal. Music by J. Nevett Steele.

Tempo di marzia.
1. From all Thy saints in war - fare, for all Thy saints at rest . . . . , To
Thee, O blessed Je - sus, all prais-es be address'd. Thou, Lord, didst win the
bat - tle, that they might conquerors be; Their crowns of living glo - ry are
divisi. rall. dim
lit with rays from Thee: Their crowns of living glory are lit with rays from Thee.

SAINT JOHN THE EVANGELIST.

5 Praise for the loved Disciple, exile on
Patmos' shore;
Praise for the faithful record he to Thy
Godhead bore;
Praise for the mystic vision, through
him to us reveal'd.
May we, in patience waiting, with Thine
elect be seal'd.

GENERAL ENDING.

19 Apostles, Prophets, Martyrs, and all the
sacred throng,
Who wear the spotless raiments, who
raise the ceaseless song;
For these, pass'd on before us, Saviour,
we Thee adore,
And, walking in their footsteps, would
serve Thee more and more.

20 Then praise we God the Father, and praise we God the Son,
And God the Holy Spirit, Eternal Three in one;
Till all the ransom'd number fall down before the throne,
And honor, power, and glory ascribe to God alone.

Hymn 334.

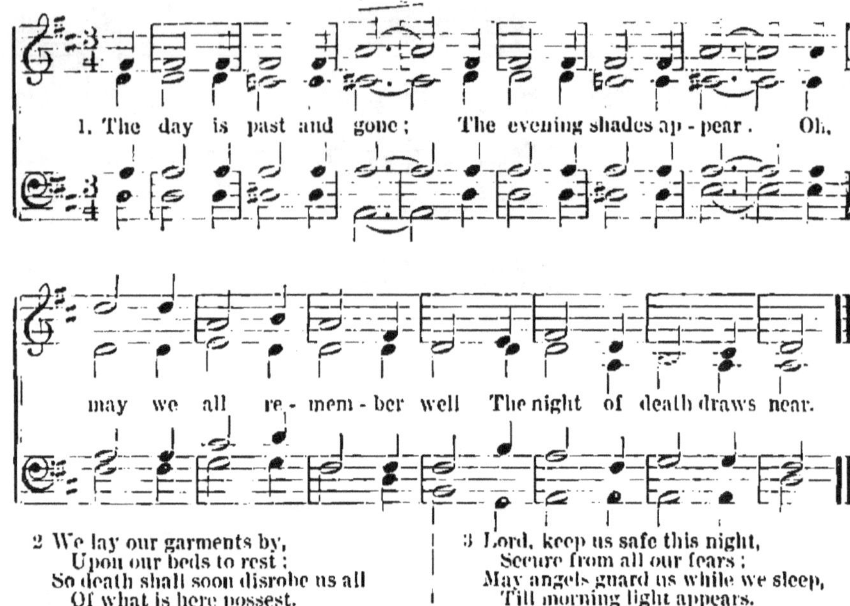
1. The day is past and gone; The evening shades ap - pear. Oh,
may we all re - mem - ber well The night of death draws near.

2 We lay our garments by,
Upon our beds to rest;
So death shall soon disrobe us all
Of what is here possest.

3 Lord, keep us safe this night,
Secure from all our fears;
May angels guard us while we sleep,
Till morning light appears.

Words from Hymnal. Music by J. NEVETT STEELE.

1. Just as I am,—without one plea, But that thy blood was shed for me, And that thou bidd'st me come to thee, O Lamb of God, I come.

2 Just as I am,—and waiting not,
To rid my soul of one dark blot,
To thee, whose blood can cleanse each [spot,
O Lamb of God, I come.

3 Just as I am,—though toss'd about,
With many a conflict, many a doubt,
Fighting and fears within, without,
O Lamb of God, I come.

4 Just as I am,—poor, wretched, blind—
Sight, riches, healing of the mind,
Yea, all I need in thee to find,
O Lamb of God, I come.

5 Just as I am,—thou wilt receive,
Wilt welcome, pardon, cleanse, relieve,
Because thy promise I believe,
O Lamb of God, I come.

6 Just as I am,—thy love unknown
Has broken every barrier down;
Now to be thine, yea, thine alone,
O Lamb of God, I come.

Hymn 392.

Second Tune. Music by J. NEVETT STEELE.

1. Just as I am,—with-out one plea, But that thy blood was shed for me, And that thou bidd'st me come to thee, O Lamb of God, I come.

Faith: Hymn 394.

Words from Hymnal. J. NEVETT STEELE.

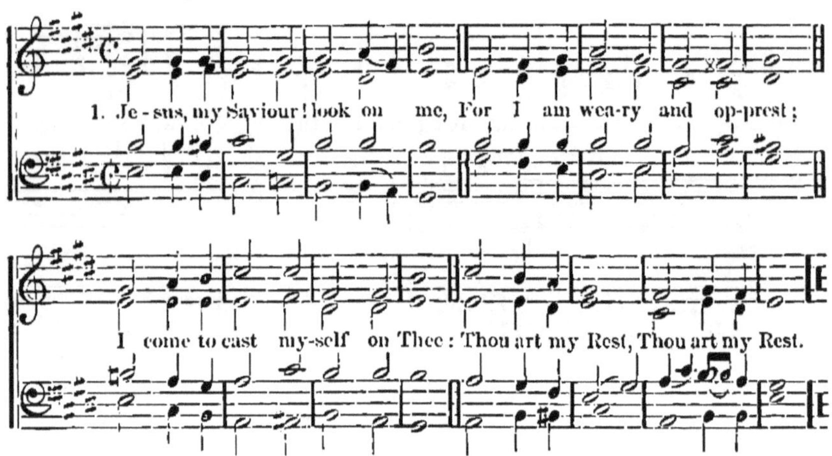
1. Je-sus, my Saviour! look on me, For I am wea-ry and op-prest;
I come to cast my-self on Thee: Thou art my Rest, Thou art my Rest.

2 Look down on me, for I am weak,
I feel the toilsome journey's length;
Thine aid omnipotent I seek;
Thou art my Strength.

3 I am bewilder'd on my way,
Dark and tempestuous is the night;
Oh, send thou forth some cheering ray:
Thou art my Light.

4 When Satan flings his fiery darts,
I look to thee; my terrors cease;
Thy cross a hiding-place imparts:
Thou art my Peace.

5 Standing alone on Jordan's brink,
In that tremendous latest strife,
Thou wilt not suffer me to sink:
Thou art my Life.

6 Thou wilt my every want supply,
E'en to the end, whate'er befall;
Through life, in death, eternally,
Thou art my All.

Hymn 394.

Second Tune. J. NEVETT STEELE.

1. Je-sus, my Saviour! look on me, For I am wea-ry and op-prest: I
come to cast my-self on Thee: Thou art my Rest.

HYMN 422.

J. N. S.

1. Songs of praise the an - gels sang; Heav'n with Hal - le - lu - jahs rang,
When Je - ho-vah's work be - gun, When He spake and it was done.
DUET.
Songs of praise a - woke the morn, When the Prince of Peace was born;
TUTTI.
Songs of praise a - rose when He Cap - tive led cap - tiv - i - ty.

2 Heaven and earth must pass away;
Songs of praise shall crown that day:
God will make new heaven and earth;
Songs of praise shall hail their birth.
And shall man alone be dumb
Till that glorious kingdom come?
No: the Church delights to raise
Psalms, and hymns, and songs of praise.

3 Saints below, with heart and voice,
Still in songs of praise rejoice;
Learning here, by faith and love,
Songs of praise to sing above.
Borne upon their latest breath,
Songs of praise shall conquer death;
Then amidst eternal joy,
Songs of praise their powers employ.

Praise. Hymn 430.

Words from Hymnal.
Music by J. NEVETT STEELE.
1 Al - le-lu - ia! song of glad-ness, Voice of ev - er - last - ing joy;
Al - le-lu - ia! sound the sweetest Heard among the choirs on high,
Hymn - ing in God's bliss-ful man-sion Day and night in - ces - sant - ly.
After each verse.
rit. molto.
Al - le-lu - ia! song of glad-ness, Voice of ev - er - last-ing joy.

2 Alleluia! Church victorious,
  Thou may'st lift the joyful strain!
Alleluia! songs of triumph
  Well befit the ransomed train.
Faint and feeble are our praises
  While in exile we remain.
    Alleluia! &c.

3 Alleluia! songs of gladness
  Suit not always souls forlorn,
Alleluia! sounds of sadness
  'Midst our joyful strains are borne;
For in this dark world of sorrow
  We with tears our sins must mourn.
    Alleluia! &c.

4 Praises with our prayers uniting,
  Hear us, blessèd TRINITY;
Bring us to thy blissful presence,
  There the PASCHAL LAMB to see,
Then to Thee our alleluia
  Singing everlastingly.
    Alleluia! &c.

Love: Hymn 458.

Words from Hymnal. Music by J. Nevett Steele.

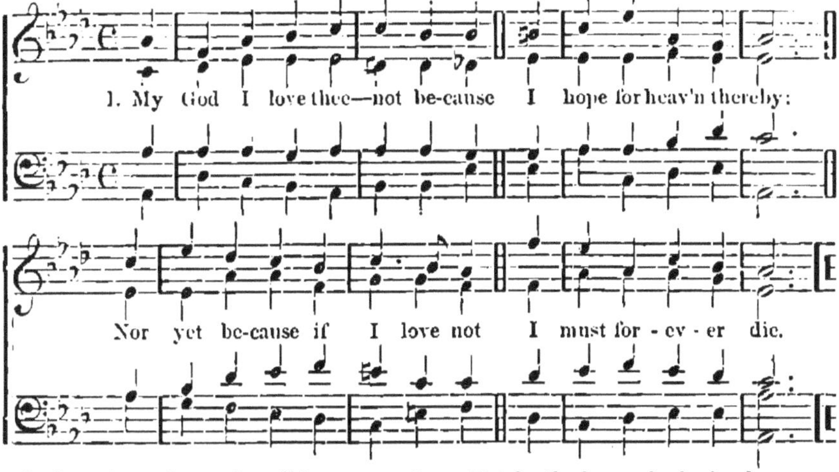

1. My God I love thee—not be-cause I hope for heav'n thereby;
Nor yet be-cause if I love not I must for - ev - er die.

2 But, O my Jesus, thou didst me
Upon the cross embrace;
For me didst bear the nails and spear,
And manifold disgrace,

3 And griefs and torments numberless,
And sweat of agony,
E'en death itself; and all for me
Who was thine enemy.

4 Then why, O blessed Jesus Christ,
Should I not love thee well?
Not for the hope of winning heaven,
Nor of escaping hell;

5 Not with the hope of gaining aught,
Not seeking a reward;
But as thyself hast loved me,
O ever-loving Lord!

6 E'en so I love thee, and will love,
And in thy praise will sing;
Solely because thou art my God,
And my eternal King.

Hymn 459

Words from Hymnal. Arranged from Schumann, by J. N. S.

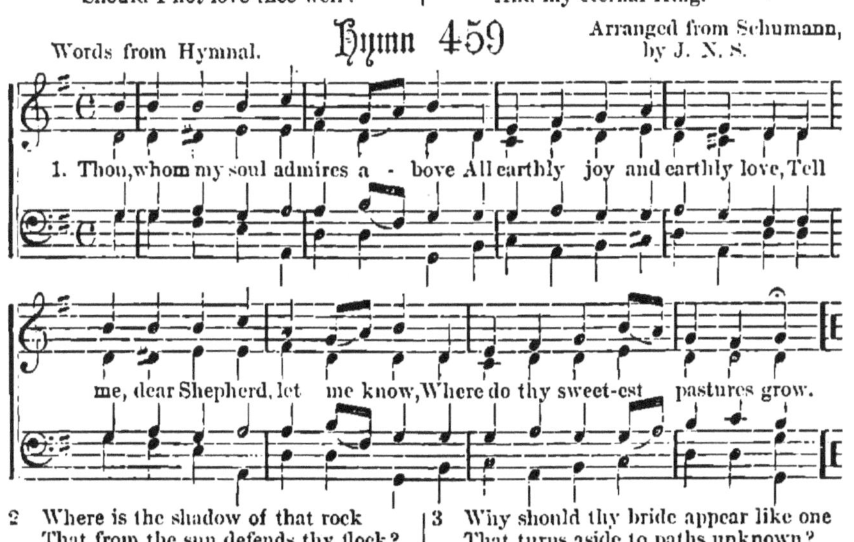
1. Thou, whom my soul admires a - bove All earthly joy and earthly love, Tell
me, dear Shepherd, let me know, Where do thy sweet-est pastures grow.

2 Where is the shadow of that rock
That from the sun defends thy flock?
Fain would I feed among thy sheep,
Among them rest, among them sleep.

3 Why should thy bride appear like one
That turns aside to paths unknown?
My constant feet would never rove,
Would never seek another love.

Dies Iræ. Hymn 483.

Words from Hymnal. Music by J. Nevett Steele.

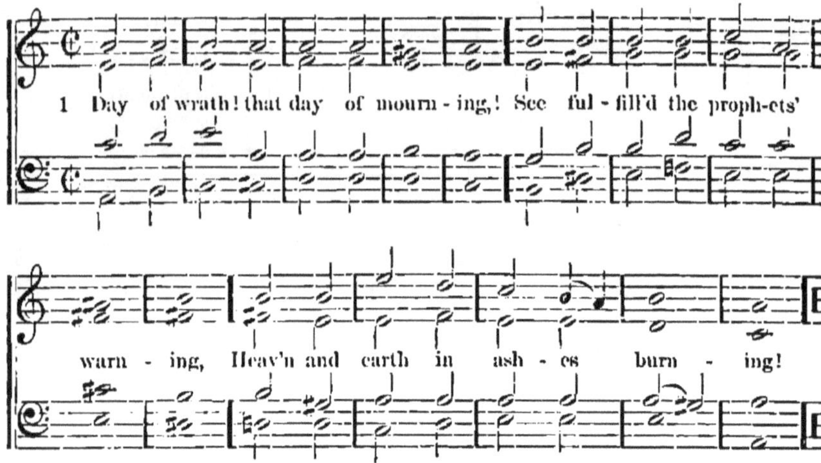
1 Day of wrath! that day of mourn - ing,! See ful - fill'd the proph-ets'
warn - ing, Heav'n and earth in ash - es burn - ing!

2 O what fear man's bosom rendeth,
When from heaven the Judge descendeth,
On whose sentence all dependeth!

3 Lo! the trumpet's wondrous swelling
Peals through each sepulchral dwelling,
All before the throne compelling.

4 Death is struck, and nature quaking,
All creation is awaking,
To its Judge an answer making.

5 Lo! the book exactly worded,
Wherein all hath been recorded:
Thence shall justice be awarded.

6 When the Judge his seat attaineth,
And each hidden deed arraigneth,
Nothing unavenged remaineth.

7 When shall I, frail man, be pleading?
Who for me be interceding,
When the just are mercy needing?

8 King of Majesty tremendous,
Who dost free salvation send us,
Fount of pity! then befriend us!

9 Think, kind Jesus, my salvation
Cost thy wondrous incarnation;
Leave me not to reprobation!

10 Faint and weary thou hast sought me,
On the cross of suffering bought me.
Shall such grace in vain be brought me?

11 Righteous Judge! for sin's pollution
Grant thy gift of absolution,
Ere that day of retribution.

12 Guilty, now I pour my moaning,
All my shame with anguish owning;
Spare, O God, thy suppliant groaning!

13 Thou the harlot gav'st remission,
Heard'st the dying thief's petition;
Hopeless else were my condition.

14 Worthless are my prayers and sighing,
Yet, good Lord, in grace complying,
Rescue me from fires undying!

15 With thy favored sheep O place me!
Nor among the goats abase me;
But to thy right hand upraise me.

16 While the wicked are confounded,
Doom'd to flames of woe unbounded,
Call me, with thy saints surrounded.

17 Bow my heart in meek submission
Strewn with ashes of contrition;
Help me in my lost condition.

18 Day of sorrows, day of weeping,
When in dust no longer sleeping,
Man awakes in thy dread keeping!

19 To the rest thou didst prepare him
By thy Cross, O Christ, upbear him;
Spare, O God, in mercy spare him.

HYMN 507.

Arranged by J. N. S.

1. Near - er my God, to thee, Near - er to thee, E'en though it
be a cross That rais-eth me; Still all my song shall be,
Near - er, my God, to thee, Near - er to thee. A - men.

2 Though like the wanderer,
Weary and lone,
Darkness comes over me,
My rest a stone;
Yet in my dreams I'd be
Nearer, my God, to thee,
Nearer to thee.

3 There let my way appear
Steps unto heaven;
All that thou sendest me
In mercy given;
Angels to beckon me
Nearer, my God, to thee,
Nearer to thee.

4 Then with my waking thoughts,
Bright with thy praise,
Out of my stony griefs
Altars I'll raise;
So by my woes to be
Nearer, my God, to thee,
Nearer to thee.

5 Or if on joyful wing.
Cleaving the sky,
Sun, moon, and stars forgot,
Upward I fly,
Still all my song shall be
Nearer, my God, to thee,
Nearer to thee.

EVENING HYMN NO. 1.

J. N. S.

1. Thee, gracious God, do we a - dore, And raise our song to Thee, And
2. For - give us, Lord, for Thy dear Son, The ill we've done this day, And

as the ev - 'ning shadows fall, We pray Thee with us be. We
for the world ourselves to Thee, We now for par - don pray. When

SOP. SOLO.

pray Thee guard us while we sleep, And let Thine an - gels vig - ils keep.
in the night we sleep-less lie, Our souls with heav'n- ly tho'ts sup - ply.

TUTTI.

And as the ev - 'ning shad-ows fall, Sweet Sav-iour, hear our call.
And as the ev - 'ning shad-ows fall, Sweet Sav-iour, hear our call.

Evening Hymn No. 2.

J. N. S.

1. Sovereign rul - er of the skies, Ev - er gra-cious, ev - er wise,
2. Times of sick-ness, times of health, Blighting want and cheer - ful wealth,

All our times are in Thy hand, All e - vents at Thy com - mand.
All our pleas - ures, all our pains, Come and end as God or - dains.

Sop. Solo.

He that formed us in the womb, He shall guide us to the tomb;
May we al - ways own Thy hand, Still to the sur - ren-dered stand,

All our ways shall ev - er be, Or-dered by His wise de - cree.
Know that Thou art God a - lone, We and ours are all Thy own.

CAROLS

A Christmas Carol.

Words by WM. AUSTIN, 1630. J. N. S.

f
All this night bright an - gels sing; Nev - er was such
f Voices in unison.
ca - rol - ling. Hark! a voice which loud - ly cries,
Mor - tals, mor - tals, wake and rise, Mor - tals, mor - tals,

A CHRISTMAS CAROL.

GIRLS.
BOYS.
wake and rise, Lo, to glad - ness, Turns your sad - ness,
GIRLS.
BOYS.

From the earth is ris'n a Sun, Shines all night though day be done.

2

Wake, O Earth, wake everything,
Wake, and hear the joy I bring,
Wake and joy; for all this night,
Heav'n and ev'ry twinkling light
All amazing
Still stand gazing;
Angels, Pow'rs, and all that be,
Wake and joy this Sun to see.

3

Hail, O Sun, O blessed Light,
Sent into this world by night,
Let thy rays and heav'nly pow'rs
Shine in these dark souls of ours,
For most duly
Thou art truly
God and man we do confess;
Hail, O Sun of Righteousness.
Amen.

WAKEN, CHRISTIAN CHILDREN!

Words by REV. S. C. HAMERTON. J. N. S.

VOICE. CHORUS.
Wak-en, Chris-tian chil-dren! Up, and let us sing
With spirit.
With glad voice the prais-es Of our new-born King.
Up! 'tis meet to wel-come, With a joy-ful lay,

WAKEN, CHRISTIAN CHILDREN!

3
3
3
3
Christ, the King of glo - ry, Born for us to - day.
3
3
3
3
3
3
Wak - en, Chris - tian chil - dren! Up, and let us sing
3
With glad voice the prais - es Of our new-born King.
FINE.
FINE.

WAKEN, CHRISTIAN CHILDREN.

This may be sung as a Solo.
1. In a man - ger low - ly Sleeps the heav'n - ly Child;
2. Come, nor fear to seek Him, Chil - dren though we be;
3. Gifts He ask - eth rich - er; Of - f'rings cost - lier still;
O'er Him fond-ly bend-eth Ma - ry, moth-er mild. Far a - bove that sta-ble,
Once He said of children, "Let them come to me." Fear not, then, to en - ter,
Yet may Christian children Bring them if they will. Brighter than all jew-els
D.C. al fine.
Up in heav'n so high, One bright star outshin-eth, Watching si - lent-ly.
Though we can - not bring Gold, or myrrh, or incense Fit - ting for a King.
Shines the mod-est eye: Best of gifts He lov - eth In - fant pu - ri - ty.

Young and Old must raise the Lay.

Words from NEALE'S SEQUENCES. J. N. S.

1. Young and old must raise the lay, That their heart en -
2. If the pur - ple proves the King, Where is good - ly
3. Josh - ua hastes to meet the foes, Boast - ful and de -
ga - ges; For the Child is born to - day,
rai - ment? If man need - eth ran - som - ing,
fi - ant; Da - vid to his breth - ren goes,
Who is King of a - ges: For the God by
Who shall make the pay - ment? For the pur - ple,
And shall slay the gi - ant: Help is nigh to

YOUNG AND OLD MUST RAISE THE LAY.

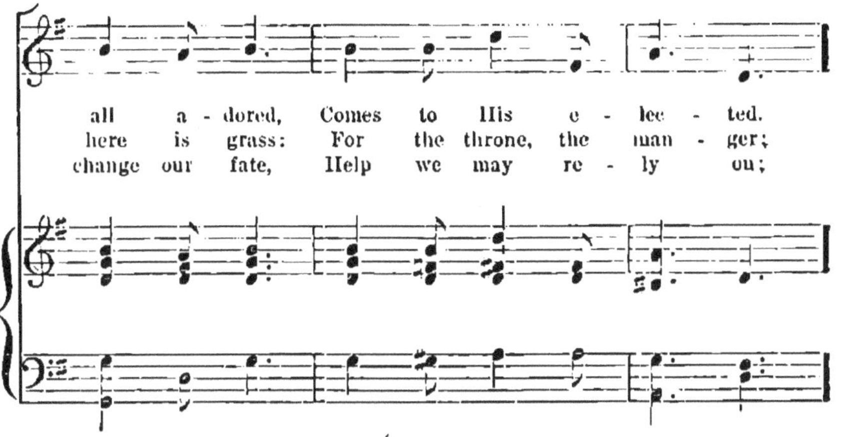
all a - dored, Comes to His e - lec - ted.
here is grass: For the throne, the man - ger;
change our fate, Help we may re - ly on;

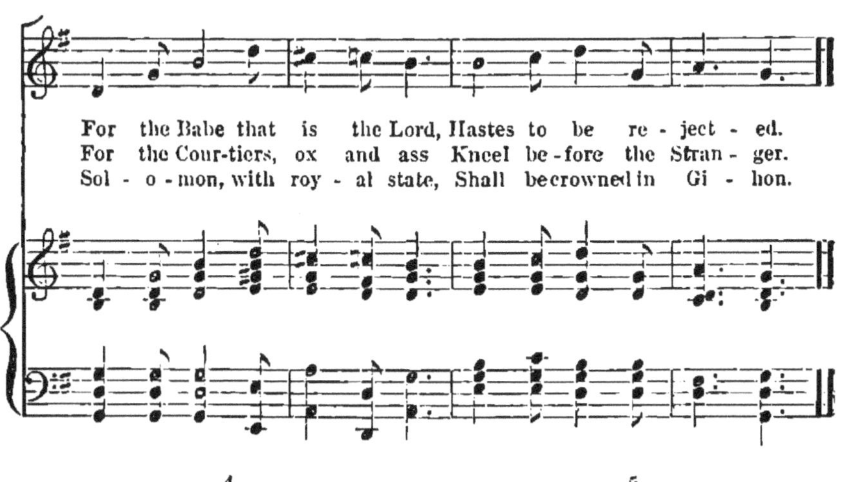
For the Babe that is the Lord, Hastes to be re - ject - ed.
For the Cour-tiers, ox and ass Kneel be-fore the Stran - ger.
Sol - o - mon, with roy - al state, Shall be crowned in Gi - hon.

4

Through the desert as we go,
  Sorrowful and fearing,
From the Rock the waters flow,
  That shall work our cheering.
Manna, wherewith all are fed,
  Comes for our Salvation;
Born in Bethlehem, "House of Bread"
  By interpretation.

5

Young and old must raise the lay
  That their heart engages;
For the Child is born to-day
  Who is King of ages:
Young and old their deeds so frame,
  That, as He comes hither,
They, when He their lives shall claim,
  May to Him go *thither*.

CHRISTMAS CAROL.

Words from the Latin. J. N. S.

1. On the birth-day of the Lord An-gels joy in glad ac-cord,
2. Born is now Em-man-u-el, He, announced by Ga-bri-el,

And they sing in sweet-est tone, Glo-ry be to God a-lone.
He, Whom prophets old at-test, Com-eth from His Fa-ther's Breast.

These good news an An-gel told To the Shepherds by their fold,
Born to-day is Christ the Child, Born of Ma-ry un-de-filed,

CHRISTMAS CAROL.

Told them of the Sav-iour's birth, Told them of the joy for earth.
Born the King and Lord we own; Glo - ry be to God a - lone.
Christ is born of maid-en fair, Christ is born of maid - en fair,
Ma - ry doth the Sav - iour bear, Ma - ry ev - er pure.

To Calvary Church Sunday School, N. Y.

On the Birthday of the Lord.

Translated from the Latin by Rev. Dr. Littledale. J. N. S.

Voice.
1. On the Birth - day of the Lord An - gels joy in
glad ac - cord, And they sing in sweet - est tone,
Glo - ry be to God a - lone.
Chorus.
Christ is born of
p

ON THE BIRTHDAY OF THE LORD.

mai - den fair, Ma - ry doth the Sav - iour bear;
Ma - ry ev - er pure, Ma - ry ev - er pure.

2 These good news an angel told
To the shepherds by their fold,
Told them of the Saviour's birth,
Told them of the joy for earth.
CHORUS.

3 Born is now Emmanuel,
He, announced by Gabriel,
He, whom prophets old attest,
Cometh from His Father's breast.
CHORUS.

4 Born to-day is Christ the Child,
Born of Mary undefiled,
Born the King and Lord we own;
Glory be to God alone.
CHORUS.

A Child this Day is born.

CHRISTMAS CAROL.

Words—Traditional.

J. N. S.

1. A child this day is born, A child of high re-

Allegro.

Voices in unison.

nown, Most wor - thy of a scep - tre, a

scep - tre and a crown.

CHORUS.

Glad ti - dings to all

A CHILD THIS DAY IS BORN.

men; . . . Glad ti - dings sing we may . . . Be -

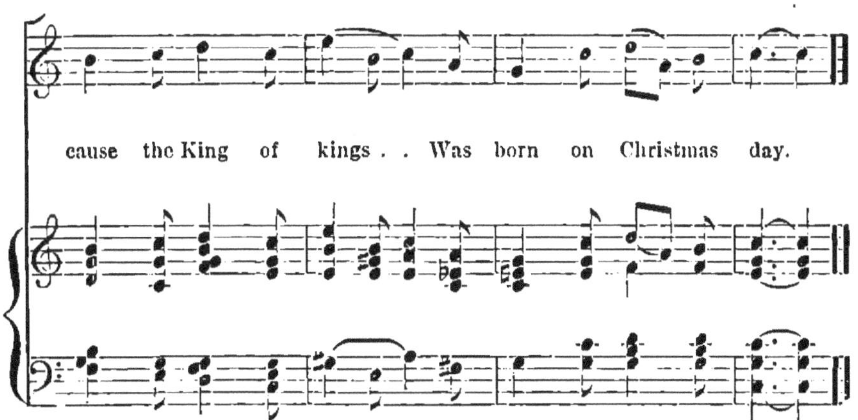
cause the King of kings . . Was born on Christmas day.

2 These tidings Shepherds heard
Whilst watching o'er their fold,
'T was by an Angel unto them
That night revealed and told.
Glad tidings, etc.

3 Then with the Angel was
An host incontinent*
Of heavenly bright soldiers,
All from the highest sent.
Glad tidings, etc.

4 They praised the Lord our God,
And our celestial King:
All glory be in Paradise,
This heavenly host do sing.
Glad tidings, etc.

5 All glory be to God,
That sitteth still on high,
With praises and with triumph great
And joyful melody.
Glad tidings, etc.

* Immediately.

To Miss Edith H. Hoadley, New York.

What Child is This?

Words by W. C. Dix. J. N. S.

1. What child is this, who, laid to rest, On Ma - ry's lap is sleep - ing? Whom an - gels greet with an - thems sweet, While shep-herds watch are keep - ing?
2. Why lies He in such low es - tate, Where ox and ass are feed - ing? Good Chris - tian, fear: for sin - ners here The si - lent word is plead - ing:
3. So bring Him in - cense, gold and myrrh, Come, peas - ant, king, to own Him: The King of kings sal - va - tion brings, Let lov - ing hearts en - throne Him.

WHAT CHILD IS THIS?

This, this is Christ, the King, Whom shep - herds guard and
Nails, spear shall pierce Him through, The cross be borne for
Raise, raise the song on high, The Vir - gin sings her
an - gels sing: Haste! haste to bring Him laud, The
me, for you: Hail! hail the Word made flesh, The
lul - la - by: Joy! joy! for Christ is born. The
Babe, the Son of Ma - ry!
Babe, the Son of Ma - ry!
Babe, the Son of Ma - ry!

When Christ was born of Mary free.

CHRISTMAS CAROL.

Words Harleian M. S. J. N. S.

Lively, with spirit.
1. When Christ was born of Ma - ry free, In
2. Herds - men be - held these An - gels bright, To
3. The King is come to save man - kind, As
4. Then, dear Lord, for Thy great grace, Grant
Beth - le - hem, that fair cit - y, The An - gels sang with mirth and glee.
them ap-pear- ing with great light, Who said God's Son is born to - night,
in th Scripture's truth we find, Therefore this song we have in mind,
us in bliss to see Thy face, That we may sing to Thy sol - ace,
"In ex - cel - sis Glo - ri - a," "In ex - cel - sis Glo - ri - a."

Chime Softly, Bells of Easter.

For Zion Church Sunday School. J. N. S. (1889.)

1. Chime soft - ly, bells of East - er, Ring out your ho - liest lay; For
2. Tri - um-phant there He's stand - ing A - mid that sa-cred throne, White
3. O Fa - ther ev - er Glo - rious, O Ev - er-last - ing Son, O
CHRIST THE LORD is ris - en, 'Tis Res - ur - rec-tion Day. The an-gels sing His
hap - py hearts are rais - ing The glad vic - to - rious song; Ye mer-ry birds, sing
Spir - it all Vic - to - rious, Thrice Ho - ly Three in One; Great GOD of our Sal -
prais - es; The gates of pearl - y white Shed o'er our gen - tle Sav - iour Pure
blithely on, Your car - ols sound a - broad; And let the liv - ing world u-nite In
va - tion, Whom earth and Heav'n adore; Praise, glo - ry, ad - o - ra - tion Be
gleams of ho - ly light. Chime soft-ly, bells of East - er, 'Tis Res-ur-rec-tion Day.
prais-es un - to God.
Thine for ev - er - more.
pp*

* Introduce Triangle here on first and third beats.

Days grow longer.

EASTER CAROL.

J. N. S., 1887.
1. Days grow long - er, sunbeams strong - er, Eas - ter tide makes all things new; Lent is ban - ish'd, sad - ness van - ish'd Christ hath ris - en, rise we too! Christmas meetings, Twelfth night greetings,
2. Earth - ly sto - ry crowns with glo - ry Him who earth - ly foes o'er - came: Vic - tor's lau - rel ends the quar - rel Hon - or dwells a - bout His name: Vanquish'd legions, conquered re-gions,
3. Then un - end - ing and trans-cend - ing Be the glo - ry of the Son; For tran-scend - ent and re - splend - ent Was the vic - t'ry He hath won! Death hath yielded, life is shielded,

DAYS GROW LONGER.

rit.
a tempo.
Whit - sun sports are glad and gay; But the light - est
Kings de - posed and princ - es bound, Ex - al - ta - tion,
Sa - tan bound, and Hell in chains: Chased is ter - ror,
rit.
and the bright - est Of our feasts is Eas - ter day.
ac - clam - a - tion Fill His ears and float a - round.
fled is er - ror, Grief is past, and joy re - mains.
rit. molto.
Hal - le - lu - jah! Bless - ed feast of Eas - ter Day!
ff
pp
ff
rit. molto.

Kyrie Eleison.

J. N. S. (1889.)

Lord have mer-cy up - on us, And in-cline our hearts to keep this law.

After the Tenth Commandment.
Lord have mer - cy up - on us, and write all these thy

laws in our hearts, we be-seech Thee, we be - seech Thee.

Ter Sanctus.

Rev. J. N. Steele.

p
cres.
Ho - ly, Ho - ly, Ho - ly, Lord God of Hosts. . . . .
p
ppp
f
Heav'n and earth are full, Heav'n and earth are full of Thy glo-ry.
3
ff
f
f
ff

p
ff
p
Glo - ry be to Thee, O Lord, O Lord most High, O Lord most High.
pp
A - men. A - men. A - - men.
pp

Shout the Glad Tidings.

Rev. J. Nevett Steele.

Allegro.
Soprano. Dec.
Can.
Tutti.
Alto.
ff
Shout the glad ti - dings, Shout the glad ti - dings, Shout the glad
Tenor.
Bass.
ti - dings, Ex - ult - ing - ly sing, Je - ru - sa - lem triumphs, Mes-
si - ah is King!
Soli.
1. Si - on the mar-vel - lous sto - ry be
2. Tell how he com - eth from na - tion to
tell - ing, The Son of the High - est how low - ly His
na - tion, The heart-cheer - ing news let the earth ech - o

SHOUT THE GLAD TIDINGS.

Tutti. cres.
birth! The bright - est Arch - an - gel in glo - ry ex -
round, How free to the faith- ful He of - fers sal -
Organ.
Tutti. cres.
cell - ing, He stoops to re - deem thee, He reigns up - on earth.
va-tion, How his peo - ple with joy ev - er - last - ing are crown'd.
Dec.
Can.
Tutti.
Shout the glad ti - dings, Shout the glad ti - dings, Shout the glad

SHOUT THE GLAD TIDINGS.

ti - dings, Ex - ult - ing - ly sing, Je - ru - sa - lem triumphs, Mes-
1st.
:S: 2d.
Soli. p
si - ah is King! King! 3. Mor-tals, your hom - age be
grate - ful - ly bring - ing, And sweet let the glad - some Ho -
Tutti. ff
san - na a - rise. Ye an - gels, the full hal - le - lu - jah be
decrescendo.
sing - ing, One cho - rus re-sound thro' the earth and the skies.

SHOUT THE GLAD TIDINGS.

Dec.
Can.
Shout the glad ti - dings, Shout the glad ti - dings,
Tutti.
Dec.
Shout the glad ti - dings, Ex - ult - ing - ly sing. Shout the glad
Can.
Tutti.
ti - dings, Shout the glad ti - dings, Shout the glad ti - dings, Ex -
ult - ing - ly sing, Ex - ult - ing - ly sing.

SHOUT THE GLAD TIDINGS.

CAN.

Shout the glad ti - dings, Ex - ult - ing - ly

DEC.

BASSI.

Je - ru - sa - lem tri - umphs, Mes - si - ah is

ORG. *Ped.*

sing, Je - ru - sa - lem tri - umphs, Mes - si - ah is

Shout the glad ti - dings, Shout the glad ti - dings,

King, ... Je -

SHOUT THE GLAD TIDINGS.

King. Shout the glad ti - dings, Ex - ult - ing - ly sing, Je -
Shout the glad
ru - sa -lem tri-umphs, Mes - si - ah is King.
- ru - sa - lem tri - umphs, Mes - si - ah is King.
ti - dings Shout the glad ti - dings,

SHOUT THE GLAD TIDINGS.

Shout the glad ti - dings, Ex - ult - ing - ly sing, Je - ru - sa-lem
Shout the glad ti - dings, Ex - ult - ing - ly sing, Je - ru - sa-lem
rit. molto pp
tri-umphs, Mes - si - ah is King, Mes - si - ah is King.
tri-umphs, Mes - si - ah is King, Mes - si - ah is King.
rit. molto
pp
ppp

INDEX.

www.ingramcontent.com/pod-product-compliance
Lightning Source LLC
Chambersburg PA
CBHW031801090426
42739CB00008B/1109

* 9 7 8 3 3 3 7 0 8 9 8 6 3 *